30 LAW OF ATTRACTION

PRACTICAL EXERCISES

By
Louise Stapely

First published December 2013

ISBN-13:978-1515110187

ISBN-10:1515110184

<u>Books by Louise Stapely</u>
<u>(LOA in Action Series)</u>

30 Law of Attraction Practical Exercises
The Power of Affirmations & the Secret to Their
Success
33 Guided Visualizations to Create the Life of Your
Dreams

Contents

Introduction

The human race has been blessed with a perfect law, a law that has the power to transform anyone's life for the better, no matter how bad it currently is. This law, called the Law of Attraction, simply states that *like attracts like* and what we think about we bring about.

For some, this concept is easy to grasp and practice, but for others, it is a little more difficult. I fall into the latter category, although not so much anymore. I discovered the Law of Attraction in 2007 when my life couldn't get any worse, it was truly a blessing for me, one that I am eternally grateful for. But it wasn't smooth sailing and certainly didn't happen overnight.

At the time of writing this, it has been 6 years since I first read about this powerful law. During 5 of those years, I started practicing the Law of Attraction dozens of times, but never persisted with it. I always compare it to vitamins and the gym! I have at least 8 nearly-full bottles of different vitamins in the cupboard, all started but never finished, and I have wasted countless expensive gym memberships, paying a ridiculous monthly fee to go twice, maybe three times. My initial Law of Attraction journey was no different. I'd buy a fancy journal (another one), write out my goals, do some visualizing when I had time, say affirmations when I remembered to, and so on. Then the usual would happen, I'd get bored or busy, and would stop. Frustratingly, this carried on for 5 years.

While I managed to move certain areas of my life forwards in positive ways, there were still several aspects of my life that made me so unhappy. At the end of 2012, I decided enough was enough. I was going to master the Law of Attraction, once and for all!

And I definitely had all the necessary tools at my disposal.

If you're anything like me, I'm sure some of you reading this will be able to open up your very own Law of Attraction libraries. I have 3 dozen books on the subject, 8 movies and countless CD's. I have read, watched, and listened to them all several times over. While the majority of my collection is fantastic and has provided me with a great understanding of the Law, I always felt it lacked a practical knowledgebase.

I have so many wonderful books telling me how amazing and miraculous the Law of Attraction is, and while I agree with them all, very few are dedicated to providing information on practical ways to manifest your desires. I'm the type of person who needs direction, I like to have a specific task to complete, in order to get me from A to B. As a result, I'm a sucker for "How To....." books! I'd love to be fabulously creative, and come up with my own ideas and ways to practice the Law of Attraction, but unfortunately that just isn't me. I need direction.

For this reason, I decided to collate all the exercises I had learned and read about over the years into one document. Having this information in one place gave me the encouragement and focus I needed to practice the Law of Attraction. What has happened in my life over the last 12 months, as a result of practicing these exercises consistently is nothing short of a miracle.

But the best thing is I created the miracle!

If I had used the Law of Attraction 6 years ago, like I have in the last 12 months, I would have avoided a lot of unhappiness and upset. However, I truly believe that life is not about past regrets, it is about looking forward. For those of you who are still unhappy with certain aspects of your life, I urge you to practice this magnificent law, once and for all. Be consistent with it. Make a promise to yourself that you will give it a proper go. What have you got to lose?

Chapter 1

My Story

Some people might think that I discovered the Law of Attraction completely by accident, others may view it as something that was meant to be. Either way, it appeared in my life at a time when I really needed it. At the time, I was in an abusive relationship, both mentally and physically. While the physical abuse scared me to death, the mental abuse damaged me on a deeper level. My self-esteem was literally non-existent, I didn't look after my appearance, I had no interest in clothes, I was always sick with the latest bug, I lost a lot of weight to the point where I was skin and bone, and my confidence had vanished. Needless to say I was deeply, deeply unhappy. To top it off, I hated my job, I had a 4 hour commute every day, I was hanging out with the wrong crowd, and I was always broke.

A friend of mine at the time, who happened to be male (I had to save him in my phone under a female name as my partner would probably have killed me), text me one day to say he had a spare ticket to a seminar in the city convention center. I said I'd go without really thinking about it, and didn't even ask what the seminar was about. When the day came I was annoyed I had agreed to go as I had had a horrible day in work, and all I wanted to do was go home and curl up under the duvet. But I went anyway. The speaker ended up being a gentleman named Wayne Dyer, I had never heard of him before. I resonated with some of what he was saying but most of it seemed to be a little out there for me. At the end of the talk, there was a large stand with several different books for sale. 2 books stood out to me, *You Can Heal Your Life* by Louise Hay, and *Ask and it is Given* by Ester & Jerry Hicks. I bought them both.

Having enjoyed my evening, I went home and immediately started reading Louise Hay's book. I was hooked. The book is about learning to love oneself, not in a conceited way, but on a deeper, more emotional level. Self-love was a lesson I definitely needed to learn.

That is the point where my life changed.

I bought several books after that, and continued to practice loving myself by doing mirror work and affirmations. Within 2 months I found the courage to leave my partner. I called my Mum and asked if myself and Harry (my dog/love of my life) could come home. She immediately said yes. It was the hardest thing I've ever had to do. I'll never forget the poor broken girl (me) getting into the car and driving away, barely able to see the road with the tears streaming down her face. But I had done it, I had taken the first step. I was scared, I was on my own, but I was free.

Shortly after, I decided to do a holistic course on massage and reflexology, while continuing to work in my crummy job as a life assurance administrator. I started to use affirmations and visualization techniques where I imagined myself working in a salon surrounded by friendly, happy people. 2 weeks after I finished the course, I was at a holistic convention where I met an old friend. Her Aunty was with her who happened to own a huge salon & spa about 30 minutes drive from me. She asked me to come and meet with her the next day as she was looking for a therapist. I did. She offered me the job on the spot. I skipped into work the next day and handed in my notice! I left my old, horrible job 30 days later.

I can't even describe how much I enjoyed my new job, I absolutely loved it. I loved the work, the loved the clients, and I loved the staff. I was so happy.

My workplace also happened to be a training center (which I didn't know before I started) for students who chose to study complementary therapies. One day my boss asked me to step in as a tutor, as the usual lady had called in sick. I was in a complete panic and so so nervous, as I had never imagined myself as a tutor before. I was completely out of my comfort zone but quickly realized that teaching was something I really loved to do. I couldn't believe the confidence it gave me. As a result, I went on to do a teaching qualification, and continued on this route for 2 years.

During that time, I regularly compiled exam questions for my students, and found them to be very successful. One day a student suggested I compile the questions into a book and self publish to make extra money. I looked into it and that is exactly what I did. At the beginning it really took off, I was making an extra $1500 - $2,000 per month. But then the recession hit, and because I wasn't regularly practising the Law of Attraction, my sales were badly affected. I continued to work while accepting my poor sales.

While my work life was really great, the one part of my life that had never gotten any better was my love life. In 2010, I was getting fed up meeting one lousy guy after another, so decided to do some Law of Attraction work on manifesting my perfect relationship. I wrote out a list of attributes I wanted my partner to have, and started to visualize meeting the man of my dreams. About 3 months later, while on holiday, I spotted this absolute gorgeous guy in the same bar I was in. After several sneaky glances, he came up to speak to me. It turned out to be the most magical time of my life, we fell head over heels in love with each other and moved in together after knowing one another for 1 month. We have now been together for 2.5 years, and are very happy. We never fight, we have the same interests, and we both support and nourish each other.

By the end of 2011, I had my perfect relationship and I was happy.......for the most part! However, I was still always broke, and worse still, the company I worked for started talking about possible cut backs in 2012. My self-published academic books were making about $300 per month, which simply wasn't enough money to allow me to leave full time work. I had several ideas for more books but desperately needed to work from home in order to complete them.

I started to read my Law of Attraction books again. After a couple of movies and books I realised I was going down the same path as I had before. Reading, watching, and listening but not enough action. Enough was enough. I spent about 3 weeks gathering practical exercises, and decided I was going to consistently practice them for 12 months. And what a year it was!

So what happened to me in 2013?

1. I now have 5 books completed and for sale on Amazon.

2. My income from my books went from $300 per month to $4,100 per month.

3. I left full time employment on 30th June 2013 and now work full time from home.

4. I am still in a happy, harmonious relationship.

5. I have lovely friends.

6. I had 3 fantastic vacations.

2013 has been my best year yet, and there is no doubt in my mind why. I practiced the Law of Attraction consistently. I had bad days, yes, but I accepted these for what they were, bad days. Everyone has them. You have to pick yourself up and continue on your quest, believing the Universe is working away behind the scenes to manifest your desires.

By having specific practical exercises to complete, I was able to focus my attention on what I wanted, and never lose faith.

My main goals for 2014:

1. Buy a bigger home together.

2. Get engaged and book my wedding.

3. Write 7 more books.

4. Increase my income to $10,000 per month.

5. Visit Hawaii, Italy and Australia.

I believe, beyond a shadow of a doubt, that I can achieve each and every one of those goals. I'm very excited!!

I started my Law of Attraction journey from a place of

complete desperation. No matter where you are, what situation you are in, who you are with, what you have, you too can manifest the life of your dreams. Always remember:

Practice, Focus, & Persistence.

Update for 2015

Hey guys!

I just thought I'd give you an update on my 2014 goals to keep you motivated and inspired on your LOA journey! I'm still consistently practicing, I hope you are too!

Sooooo, my goals for 2014....

1. Buy a bigger home together – check! We now live in a beautiful house in an area that I love.

2. Get engaged and book my wedding – I got engaged....woohoo! This was a big deal for me as my fiancé didn't really believe in marriage and was never interested in it. That has totally changed now, he is like a different person. Regarding the wedding....well we did have it booked for 2015 BUT I fell pregnant in December 2014 so we have postponed it until 2016. Our little bundle of joy is due to arrive on the 3rd of September 2015, 7 weeks to go. We are both so happy and bursting with excitement!

3. Write 7 more books – I only completed 5 books in 2014 but with very good reason. I started a degree in Nutritional Therapy (I have wanted to do this for so long) in September 2014 and have just recently completed year 1. I adore the course. It has taken up a lot of my time, hence I only got 5 books completed, but it is totally worth it, and will definitely help me with further books/projects in the future.

4. Increase my income to $10,000 per month – my income as at December 2014 was averaging $9,247 per month. Not exactly $10,000 but I'm not complaining!

5. Visit Hawaii, Italy, and Australia – thankfully we got to visit Hawaii and Italy, which were spectaculor but Australia will have to wait until our little baby arrives.

I'm really happy with what I have achieved over the last year and a half. Its still a journey though, and I'm still learning. I continue to read my favorite LOA books from time to time to keep myself motivated.

My goals for the rest of 2015:

1. Start a nutrition/juicing blog.

2. Be the best Mum I can be.

3. Continue with year 2 of my college course, and do well.

4. Finish 1 more book before the baby arrives.

I wish so much success and happiness for everybody. Please believe you can achieve it because I promise you, you can.

Chapter 2

How To Use The Exercises

There are 30 exercises provided in this book, some you will enjoy, and some you will find pointless. I can't tell you which exercises to choose, this is something very personal to you. My one piece of advice is not to do all 30 together, this will become a chore and that is something you need to avoid. Choose the exercises that resonate with you, ones that make you feel comfortable. If you don't enjoy it, don't do it. If you do enjoy it, then do it. It's as simple as that.

I have used all exercises at one time or another but the ones that I use regularly are:

- ❖ Exercise 1 - Movie Magic
- ❖ Exercise 2 - Attitude of Gratitude
- ❖ Exercise 5 - It's Raining Money
- ❖ Exercise 7 - Visualization
- ❖ Exercise 16 – Affirmations
- ❖ Exercise 28 - Tap to Success

When I started this experiment at the beginning of 2012 I used most of the money exercises to begin with, because that was my main goal - to increase my income.

It all depends on what your goals are. If you have plenty of money but would love to get married, then Exercises 1, 7, and 25 would be a great place to start.

I haven't listed the exercises in any order of importance. I honestly don't believe one is more important than the other. My top 6 are the ones I have listed at the beginning of this chapter, they won't necessarily be your top 6.

I would advise you read through each exercise, twice if you can. Get a feel for what is required and how comfortable you feel about practicing it.

I wish you every success in the world. Know now, whatever it is you desire is on its way to you. You just have to believe it. Practice it. Focus on it. Persist with it. Your dreams will come true, as they have done for me.

For the rest of the book, I have referred to the Law of Attraction as the LOA.

Chapter 3

Practical Exercises

Exercise 1

Movie Magic

Both gratitude and mind movies are LOA power houses as far as I'm concerned, but personally the one that has had, and continues to have the most emotional effect on me, is mind movies.

When I finish watching my movie my heart is racing, I'm feeling excited and pumped, I'm smiling, and most importantly, I'm so so motivated. No matter how many books you read on the LOA, the number one constant in all of them is feeling or emotion. There is no point visualizing having your perfect body with absolutely no emotion behind it. It is a waste of time. You need to feel excited about your toned, lean new look, feel confident when walking down the street, feel beautiful, healthy, and strong. I truly believe the number one way to supercharge your emotions is to create a mind movie for whatever desire you have.

So, what is a mind movie?

It is basically an audio-visual method of visualization, similar to a vision board, but instead of being on a scrap board it is on your computer/TV screen. How neat is that?! A mind movie is a collection of powerful photos and images (chosen by you) reinforced with positive affirmations (chosen by you), all shown on a digital screen with emotionally motivating music in the background.

Emotionally motivating = the key to success!

Let's use wealth as an example:

So many people (including myself) really struggle with sitting in a quiet room, closing their eyes, and visualizing being rich. How do you visualize being rich? It's easy for some, but for me my mind wanders after a few seconds.....did I take the chicken out of the freezer for dinner......I should have bought those black shoes, they were a bargain......maybe I'll have time to go get them tomorrow....arrrrgh I need to focus! Before I know it, there is an internal battle going on in my head between my meditating mind and my every day, normal mind. At this point I usually give up, feeling frustrated and deflated. Thankfully mind movies have taken all the stress out of visualizing for me. By watching my movie every day, I stay focused on my goals and desires, while the universe continues to find glorious ways to make my dreams come true, literally! I will show you how to create your own mind movie further along in this chapter but first, here are some tips on how to make that perfect movie.

How long should my mind movie be?

My first mind movie was 8 minutes long, it was basically the length of 3 songs. I watched it for a while but on some occasions, by the end of song 2, I found myself looking at my watch or thinking about what I was going to do next. Totally counterproductive. I shortened it into 1 song which was about 3 minutes and 20 seconds long, and found it held my attention and focus more effectively. Also, the excited feeling I had at the end of the movie was much more sustainable throughout my day. Therefore I would recommend anywhere between 3 and 4 minutes, nothing longer. I usually use the length of the song as a guideline.

Where do I get images and photos for my mind movie?

The great thing about creating your own mind movie is that you can use actual photos of yourself, your friends, your family members, your significant other, your dog, your cat, anybody you choose. Upload these photos from your camera or Smartphone onto your computer and save into a folder. I like to name my folders for a specific desire, for example, Money Movie, Love Movie, Car Movie, House Movie, Travel Movie.

Using property as an example, let's say you'd love to live in an oceanfront property in Malibu.
Open up Google, and type in the following search term

(**do not** put in the quotation marks):

"oceanfront property in Malibu"

Instead of searching the web, click on the word "images", this will bring up the most breathtaking, beeeeautiful pictures of various properties with blue skies, white sand, candlelit balconies etc. I bet looking at these will get your blood pumping! You can search for literally anything you want - country properties, beach properties, LA mansion, BMW, Austin Martin, Audi R8, 50" flat screen TV, Rolex watch....the list is endless!

When you find an image you like, click on it (it will become larger on the screen), then right click on the image and choose "Save Image As". Name your image and save it in the folder you created.

Recommendation: when you hover the cursor over each picture on Google (it turns into a little hand), you will see the image dimensions on the bottom of the picture. Always choose images that are higher than 500 x 500. If you use pictures with lower dimensions the image can sometimes be blurry on your movie. You don't want that, you want nice clear images!

How do I find music for my mind movie?
This is a very important step in your mind movie making. The song is going to supercharge your

emotions, and make you feel love or happiness, excitement or joy, peace or harmony, whatever positive emotion you choose. You certainly don't want to feel hurt, anger, pain, fear, sadness, or boredom so I'd probably avoid Metallica or Megadeth!

Your song choice also depends on the type of movie you want to make. For example, I have a movie for marriage that shows photos of myself and my boyfriend happy together, the hotel I want to get married in, photos of beautiful wedding dresses, flowers, diamond rings, and exotic honeymoon vacations. My song choice is *From This Moment On* by Shania Twain. I love it. When I watch the movie I feel like I am actually at my wedding, and that is EXACTLY how you should be feeling. I have just started watching it and know wholeheartedly that the Universe is working behind the scenes to manifest my perfect wedding day.

If you want a new car then choose a great driving song. I love *Free Falling* by Tom Petty. If you want a new house then choose a happy, uplifting song, one that gets your heart beating fast, my song choice for that movie is *What You Get is What You See* by Tina Turner. You can literally pick any song in the world.

So let's move on with the fun bit!

How do I make my mind movie?

There are various software packages available on the internet that you can purchase and start working on, but they come at a price. I have actually discovered a great system which is 100% free (and legal!), one that enables me to build as many mind movies as I want, and have a fun time doing so. Anyone can do this, all you need to have is an internet connection, a computer/laptop/tablet, and a couple of hours free time. The longest part of the process is actually gathering the pictures, affirmations, and the song you want to include in your movie. The rest is a breeze and takes only about 20 minutes. I will go through the download and set up step by step so you can start using this incredible visualization tool today!

Step One

The system we are going to work with is called Photo Story 3. It is a free download from Microsoft and can be accessed as follows:

Open Google, and type in 'microsoft download center photo story 3' into the search field (do not use the quotation marks).

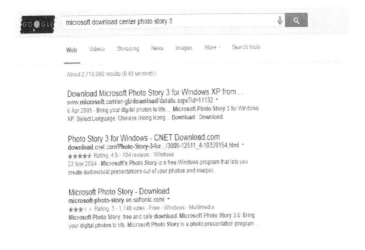

Open the very first result that appears at the top of Google (I have taken a snapshot of it so you can see what it should look like). It should say:

Download Microsoft Photo Story 3 for Windows XP from......

*If this does not work, put the following into your browser:

www.microsoft.com/en-gb/download/details.aspx?id=11132

For the purpose of this tutorial I am using Windows. If you have a Mac you cannot download Photo Story 3, but iPhoto is just as good at creating slideshows with music.

On the first screen you will see "Microsoft Photo Story

3 for Windows XP", underneath that you can select the language you prefer (default is always English), click on the red/orange box that says "Download".

A dialog box will appear which asks, "Do you want to run this file?". Click on "Run" at the bottom of the box. You will see another dialog box flash up on the screen that says "preparing to install....."

A dialog box with the title "Photo story 3 for Windows Setup Wizard" will appear. Follow the set up instructions by clicking on "Next", accept the terms of condition, and click on "Next". Click on "Next" again, and then click on "install", then click on "Finish".

And that's it. All in all it should take about 3 or 4 minutes for the whole process from beginning to end.

Sometimes the software opens automatically after installation but if it doesn't, click on your start menu and type in "photo story 3" in the box at the bottom (where it says "search programs and files). When you locate it, open it, and start building your first mind movie!

Note: I tried to download this software onto my iPad but it didn't work. The message I got was as follows:

"This download is not available on mobile devices."

While this doesn't particularly bother me because I have my laptop, those of you who would prefer to use your tablets or mobiles (iPads/iPhones) can use iPhotos. For other tablet/smartphone brands, you can build your mind movie on your PC or laptop, and transfer it to your device for viewing if you so wish.

Step 2

Now that your software is open, click on "Begin a new story", click on "next" to be directed to the next page.

Step 3

This is where you are going to upload the photos and images you want in your story. Click on "Import Pictures", find the folder where you saved all your photos. When choosing my photos I like to be able to actually see what image I'm selecting. In order to be able to do this, change the "View Menu" icon (at the top of the dialog box) to "Thumbnail". This way you can see the photos you are selecting.

You can upload one image at a time which is fine. However if you prefer to upload several images together, select the first image you want to include, hold down the "Ctrl" button and then click on all the other pictures you wish to choose. When finished, click "OK". You will now see all your pictures displayed at the bottom of the slideshow on Photo Story.

In order to remove the black borders (recommended)

from around your photos, click on "Remove Black Borders" (you will find this underneath "Import Pictures"), click "Yes to All", then click "OK".

Before we move onto the next step, if you want to move the images around, just click, hold, and drag the picture to the position you want it. You can also delete any photos by clicking on the "X" on the right hand side of the slideshow.

When you are ready to move on, click "Next".

Step 4

This is where you add your affirmations. You can have affirmations on all images or just one image, it's entirely up to you. I normally have my affirmations on every 5th photo. Choose what photo you want your affirmation to be on by selecting that image at the bottom. Write out your affirmation in the box to the right of the photo you have selected. Depending on your photo, you can have your affirmation on the top center of the screen, bottom center of the screen, or the center of the screen, just play around with it.

When choosing a photo for your affirmation, make sure it is bright so you will be able to read the affirmation. Do this for all images and then move onto the next step by clicking "Next".

Step 5

With this step you can narrate your affirmations. I skip

this bit as I don't like the sound of my own voice! I prefer motivating music.

If you decide to go ahead with narrating your own movie, select the photo you wish to narrate over. Click on the record button (the large button with the red circle in the middle) and say what you want to say. To stop, click on the button next to record (smaller circle with a blue square in the middle). Continue with this step until you have narrated over your chosen photos.

If you choose to skip this part, just click on "Next" to continue.

Step 6

This is where you will add your music! Click on "Select Music". Find the song you wish to use in your movie, select it, and click "Open". The song will now upload onto your movie.

Once you have your music uploaded, click on "Preview". You can now see what your movie looks like!!

Because you want your images to coincide with the length of the song, you may need to play around with this step. Delete photos if the song ends before the images finish, or if the images end before the song, then add more pictures.

You can always go back and alter any step by clicking on "Back". Make sure you save your project by clicking on "Save Project".

Step 7

When you have tweaked everything, it's time to build your movie. Click on "Next". Decide where you would like to save your story. Do you want to be able to view it on your PC? Smartphone? Email? I always save it to my computer but it's up to you (by default it always chooses this option). Now specify where you would like to save it, and what you would like to call the movie. Mine automatically saves into my Videos folder. Once you have followed those steps, click "Next".

The software works its magic, builds your movie, and now you can view it! Click on "View Your Story" and start manifesting!

Tips on Mind Movies

❖ You can build as many movies as you want but I would recommend concentrating on one subject at a time. If you are trying to manifest a car, a house, a partner, and good health all at once, it might get a little overwhelming, and that's when the process starts to become a chore. It must always be fun for you.

❖ I like to watch my movie first thing in the morning as it sets me up for the day. Make sure you are on your own in a quiet room. Either leave your phone in another room or switch it off, no distractions!

❖ I love watching my movie on the TV. I have saved it onto a USB Key, and plug it into the TV when I'm in the house on my own. There is something exhilarating about watching it on the big screen!

❖ Keep it short, the length of one song is plenty.

❖ If you decide to put your mind movie up on You Tube, please be aware that you cannot play certain songs due to licensing agreements. If you do, You Tube will just blank out the song.

Mind Movie Examples

I understand that some people may not have the time straight away to do something like this. If that's the case, don't panic. There are literally hundreds of mind movies on You Tube. I don't like viewing these because they are not personal to me. I would definitely recommend spending the time to build your own as you want the movie to resonate with your soul! However, in the meantime, if you log onto You Tube and key in the following terms:
"wealth mind movies"

"weight loss mind movies"

"new care mind movies"

"love mind movies"

"relationships mind movies"

"happiness mind movies"

"money mind movies"

Exercise 2

Attitude of Gratitude

"Thank You" are the two most powerful words in the Universe because they emanate gratitude and appreciation for what is received or experienced in our lives. The LOA states that what we think about, we bring about. Another fantastic way of looking at it is:

What we thank about, we bring about.

So many of us are waiting for big things to happen in our lives in order to be grateful, sometimes overlooking what is already there. Everybody has something to be grateful for, regardless of how much is in their bank account. I read a book called Gratitude by Rhonda Byrne and absolutely love the following paragraph:

If you practice gratitude a little, your life will change a little. If you practice gratitude a lot every day, your life will change dramatically and in ways that you can hardly imagine.

Those words are very powerful, and so true.

For me, practicing gratitude has had a profound effect on my life. I write in my journal every single day and always find something to be grateful for, even if it is just for the beautiful sunset.

Buy a journal, and every morning, make a list of ten blessings in your life that you are grateful for. Here are some examples:

❖ I am so happy and grateful that I had a lovely meal last night, it was absolutely delicious.

❖ I am so happy and grateful that I was able to sit in the exit row on my flight yesterday.

❖ I am so happy and grateful for experiencing the warmth of the sun today.

❖ I am so happy and grateful for the compliment Mike gave me this morning.

Even if you feel that you don't have much to be grateful for right now, there is always something you can find:

❖ I am so happy and grateful that I have paper to write my wonderful blessings each day.

❖ I am so happy and grateful that I have eyes to see the world.

- ❖ I am so happy and grateful that I have a house to live in.

- ❖ I am so happy and grateful that I have clean water to drink every day.

If you are practice gratitude throughout your day, you will draw to you, more instances and experiences to be grateful for, and wondrous things will start to happen in your life.

"Gratitude feels so good because it is the state of mind closest to your natural state in which you were born to live." - Abraham-Hicks

"Be thankful for what you have; you'll end up having more. If you concentrate on what you don't have, you will never, ever have enough." - Oprah Winfrey

Exercise 3

Mirror, Mirror on the Wall

Over the years I have attempted this practice more times than I care to admit. Of all the exercises in this book, it was the one I found the most difficult.

The teaching of self-love has been pioneered by Louise Hay for many years, and to this day, she continues to emphasize the power of learning to love oneself. Louise believes self-love is the prerequisite to attracting happiness, health, love, and abundance into your life, and I wholeheartedly agree with her.

To carry out this exercise, simply stand in front of the mirror (make sure you are on your own and will not be interrupted), look into your eyes, and out loud, say:

I love you (your name), you're perfect the way you are.

When I did this first, I was so embarrassed and couldn't look into my eyes for very long. I felt really stupid and uncomfortable.

But why?

If we can love others, then why not ourselves?

In one way I was deeply shocked by my initial reaction but in another, I felt relieved at knowing what I needed to change. I did this exercise for a couple of days on and off for about 4 years. When I finally decided to take it seriously I did it for 30 days running, and had amazing results. While initially embarrassed and uncomfortable, after about 1 week I started to feel more relaxed and at ease when I said it. I started to feel calmer and more peaceful, more confident in my ability to manifest my desires, more confident as a person, and much more at ease with others. Not only that but little things started to go my way - I never had to queue anywhere anymore, I always met happy, kind people, the traffic always went my way, and my relationships started to change for the better.

This exercise takes about 30 seconds to 1 minute so there are no excuses. Start it today. Right now, put this book down. Go into your bathroom, close the door, stand in front of the mirror, and start learning to love yourself.

I truly believe self-love is the most important law of attraction exercise you can do. It begins with I love you, 3 simple but very powerful words.

Exercise 4

Ditch the Cards, Carry the Cash

This practical exercise is like Marmite, you're either going to love it or hate it! I'm still on the fence but I'm starting to see some substance behind it.

I read a story once about a gentleman who worked in a job he didn't particularly like, he was on an average salary, had 3 kids, and was mortgaged up to the hilt, but yet he always seemed to have money. On the flip side of the coin, his friend, an electrical engineer, was on a good salary, was married but had no children, and lived in an average house with a manageable mortgage (or what is considered to be a manageable mortgage) but yet he owed thousands of dollars on credit card debt and continuously struggled for money.

The writer of the article came to this conclusion: The first man always, without fail, carried cash in his wallet in bundles of $20, $50 and some $100 notes. He seldom used credit cards and very rarely even brought them out with him.

The second man never carried cash, not a cent. He used his credit and debit cards for absolutely everything. His wallet was always empty of cash.

The LOA states that "like attracts like". The first man's wallet is always bulging with cash. The second man's wallet is always empty. What message is each man giving the universe do you think?

This was a light bulb moment for me for one simple reason. My boyfriend is quite negative when it comes to money, he is very careful with it, he doesn't impulse buy, very rarely spends anything on himself, and sometimes worries about losing his job and not being able to pay the bills. But yet he has just over $20k in a savings account, $15k in stocks and shares, 2 houses that he lets out and makes a profit on, and he always has a buffer of $3k in his debit account. This used to baffle me.....until I read that article.

My boyfriend's wallet is always bulging with cash, he uses it for everything. He only ever uses his credit card to pay for flights or something online (so he is protected).

I was the opposite, I never used cash for anything, my wallet forever looked pathetic! I actually used to smile to myself and feel sorry at how empty and sad my wallet looked. What a dreadful message to give the Universe!!

I now carry about $200 (I started off with $50) in my wallet at all times, and when I spend it I take more out to replace it. It really works too, my wallet looks healthy which makes me feel happy and secure. As long as I continue to feel those positive feelings towards my wallet then I will continue to carry cash on me at all times.

There is obviously a degree of risk with this exercise. If you lose your wallet or it gets stolen you will more than likely never see the cash again. That is why, if you decide to try this exercise, you need to carry an amount that is comfortable with you. If I were to carry $2,000 around with me every day I'd drive myself crazy with worry and again, what message is that sending out to the Universe? *Steal my wallet!*

If you have a great imagination you can always carry around Monopoly money and pretend your wallet is bulging with the real deal!

Exercise 5

It's Raining Money

This is a really fun visualization technique. It is super simple to do yet, very effective. Even if you are like me and find visualization difficult, this could be the exercise for you.

Simply put, visualize money falling out of the sky, visualize it everywhere - heaped on the chair, piled high on the bed, falling out of cupboards, absolutely everywhere!

I do this exercise when I get into bed and switch off the light (I don't fall asleep straight away). It takes about 3 to 5 minutes but you can make it as long as you wish. Because I struggle with visualization, I actually talk myself (in my head) through the process.

My script goes something like this:
"I am standing in my bedroom. I feel happy and content. I am surrounded by $20 bills, they are falling all around me, and it's raining money. I look to my right and there are thousands of $20 bills on the windowsill, I open the washing basket and it is filled high with $20 bills, they are everywhere. I can hear the swishing of the money as I walk towards the hallway, I can feel the paper bills at my feet. I

*open my wardrobe and $20 bills fall out onto the floor.
Money is gently raining down on me. As I walk past the
bathroom I see money piled high in the sink, falling out
onto the floor, I walk in and open the shower door, $20
bills fall out onto the floor, there are literally thousands of
them everywhere. I walk out into the hallway, stand tall,
and looking up to the ceiling I close my eyes. I stretch my
arms out, I can feel the $20 bills gently falling on my face,
I can smell the money, I love the smell of money. I catch
some money in my hands, look down and open my eyes. I
smile as I see the money, I love it, it looks so amazing. I
carry on down the hallway towards the main living area.
As I walk past the airing cupboard, I open the door.
Thousands of $20 bills fall out onto the floor, literally
thousands of them. I walk towards the living area, and
feel the swish of the dollar bills at my feel, I can smell the
money all around me. I feel exhilarated, I feel safe. When
I get to the living area, I stop, close my eyes, and take
several deep breaths while repeating the words, I love
money. I can feel the money gently fall on my face, gently
fall on my shoulders, my arms, my hands. There is money
everywhere, on the couch, on top of the TV, on the
bookshelf, piled high on the coffee table, covering the entire
floor, heaped on top of the kitchen counter. I open the
fridge door, thousands of $20 bills fall out of the fridge
onto the floor. I open the oven door, thousands of $20 bills
fall out onto the floor. I smile. As I return to my bed,
through the large piles of money, I know for sure that I
have enough money to have an amazing life, I can buy
whatever I choose, I can help others, I am secure, I am
financially free. As I relax in my comfortable, warm bed, I*

drift off into a wonderful sleep, full of pleasant dreams while it continues to rain $20 bills around me".

And that's it! The idea of this exercise is to get your mind's eye used to seeing lots of money. Don't forget, your subconscious believes what it is told. If you regularly see lots of money, then that is what will manifest for you.

Tips:

1. You can play a song on your iPod while you are doing this visualization technique. I recommend a nice, relaxing song, especially as you want to drift off into a lovely sleep at the end.

2. Before you get into bed, take some money in your hand and smell it, close your eyes, and move the money about in your hand. Remember how it feels, how it smells.

3. You can literally imagine raining money at any stage during the day. If you are stuck in traffic, imagine money falling from the sky around you. If you are queuing for lunch or in the bank, imagine it raining money.

4. You don't have to use $20 bills, use whatever denomination you feel comfortable with.

Exercise 6

Blank in the Bank

Doing this exercise was the most fun I've had with the LOA!

How effective it will be depends on whether you have online or paper bank statements. Online statements are much better but it will still work if you have paper only.

Online Bank Statements

Open up your most recent bank statement. Mine are always PDF documents and I'm assuming this is the case for most banks. Align the statement so that you see the date, your account number, sort code, IBAN code, your address, and balance. Now make a copy of what you can see on the screen by clicking on the print screen button on your keyboard. The button will have "Prt Sc" written at the top. Mine is at the very top of the keyboard beside F12.

When you click on this button it literally takes a photo of the screen as you are looking at it.

Now next step, open Paint on your computer. If you do not have an icon for this on your start up menu or desktop, simply open your start up menu (lower left hand corner icon) and at the bottom where it has an empty box that says "search programs and files", type in the word "Paint". You will see a small picture of a paint palette and paint brush with the word *paint* beside it, click on this and it will open onto a blank screen. At the top left hand corner, click on "Paste".

You will now see your bank statement in all its glory!

Align the statement on the screen so you can see all relevant details.

What we are going to do is erase your current balance and put in a new balance! In order to do this, select the Eraser tool at the top of the screen (it is a picture of an actual eraser, a pink one). When you have selected Eraser, hover your cursor over the details you want to erase on your bank statement, and click until it disappears (make sure you don't erase any lines or words, it needs to look as believable as possible).

When everything is erased it is time to key in your new balance...the fun bit!

How much do you want in your account? $25,000? $57,000? $160,000? $1,200,000? The choice is yours! Whatever you decide, click on the "Text" button at the top of the screen, it looks like a capital A. Then click on where you wish to write in your new balance. You might need to align the balance, and always make sure the font size is set at 12 or 14 so you can see it clearly.

When this step is completed, click Save As, and name your file (make sure you save it as a JPEG picture).

If you have a vision board (recommended), print off your new bank statement, and look at it with glee all day long!

If you work at your computer or laptop a lot (like me) then this is THE perfect screen saver.

Important tip: if you are going to use this as your screen saver, save it into a folder **on its own**, nothing else.

How to change your screen saver:
I'm using Windows as an example here but I'm sure Mac is just as easy.

1. Open the Control Panel on your PC.
2. Click on Appearance & Personalization.
3. Under the heading Personalization, click on "Change Screen Saver".
4. Choose "Windows Live Photo Gallery" from the dropdown menu.
5. Click on "Settings".
6. Make sure "Use photos & videos from C:/users.........." is selected. Click on "Browse".
7. Find the folder your bank statement is saved in. Select this folder and click "OK".
8. Beside "Use this theme", select "Classic" from the drop down menu (it is usually the first choice). This

will ensure your bank statement stays static on the screen.

9. "Slide show speed" is irrelevant once you have selected "Classic" in point 8. Choose "slow" if you have to pick one.

10. Click "Save".

Hey Presto!!

Now every time your screen saver comes on, you can see your bank balance!

Paper Bank Statements

Take out your latest paper statement, and tippex out the balance. Make sure it is very neatly done. When the tippex has completely dried, write in your new bank balance with black pen.

This won't look as real as having the online statement but it is still effective. Tape it to your bedside locker or vision board, somewhere where you will see it several times a day.

Exercise 7

Visualization

"The body is very important, but the mind is more important than the body." - Arnold Schwarzenegger

Visualization is an integral part of the creation process. It is a way to create what you want by using your imagination, by picturing yourself having or doing the things you wish to have or do. With visualization there are no limits to what you can achieve, what you can have, or who you can become. Every human being on this planet has the ability to visualize, whether they know it or not. The key to success is learning to visualize, not be default, but on purpose.

Most people have never learned to control their visualization power. Have you ever heard a rumor in work that there may be cutbacks? Before you know it, in your mind you've lost your job, house, car, you're divorced, penniless, and homeless...all because you let your imagination run riot! You must learn to control it, to visualize in a positive manner.

The key to visualization is using your imagination to see

yourself as already being in that perfect job or having that high bank balance or being happily married.

Always imagine the end result, always!

Actors/actresses, Olympic medallists, famous athletes, Fortune 500 CEO's, musicians, the list could go on and on....they've all used visualization to achieve their goals.

Arnold Schwarzenegger, five-time winner of Mr. Universe, successful movie star, real estate tycoon, and multimillionaire credits visualization as the key to his success. *"When I was very young, I visualized myself being and having what it was I wanted. Mentally I never had any doubts about it. The mind is really so incredible. Before I won my first Mr. Universe, I walked around the tournament like I owned it. The title was already mine. I had won it so many times in my mind that there was no doubt I would win it. Then I moved on to the movies, the same thing. I visualized myself being a successful actor and earning big money. I could feel and taste success. I just knew it would all happen"*

Jack Nicklaus, considered by many to be the best golfer of all time, won a phenomenal 18 Master Championships. In his book, *Golf My Way*, Nicklaus writes about using visualization before every shot he took, *"It's like a color movie. First I 'see' the ball where I want it to finish, nice and white and sitting up high on the bright-green grass. Then the scene quickly changes and I 'see' the ball going there; it's path, trajectory, and shape, even its behavior on landing. Then there is sort of a fadeout, and the next scene shows me making the kind of swing that will turn the previous image into a reality...."*

If you ever required proof that the LOA is the real deal then maybe this next story might be exactly what you need. It was certainly a turning point in my LOA journey. After reading about this lady I remember having the most magical feeling, one of confirmation like this LOA stuff might actually work. I thought "Well if she can do it, so can I". That was a big deal for me as I'm the type of person who likes to see things on paper, I like to see proof and I like to see proven results!

Cynthia Stafford, a resident of California, won $112 million in the California Mega Millions in 2007. Wow, wasn't she lucky I hear you ask? Well, to answer your question, no she wasn't. Luck had nothing to do with it. Four months before her big lottery win, Cynthia decided that she was going to win $112 million. She wrote that **exact figure** on a piece of paper, meditated on it, visualized what she would buy with it, felt how it would feel to hold that check in her hand, kept the piece of paper under her pillow and looked at it every single night before she went to bed.

Cynthia did this for 4 months.

While Cynthia found it difficult in the beginning to be disciplined in her approach, she was determined to continue. After reading *The Power of Your Subconscious Mind* by Joseph Murphy, she believed so strongly in the power of the mind, she just knew she had to continue manifesting the lottery win.

On Mother's Day in 2007, Cynthia bought a $2 lottery ticket and won. The most amazing part of this incredible story is that Cynthia won $112 million, the EXACT amount she wrote down 4 months previous. *"I knew I'd get here,"* Stafford says, *"It was just a matter of visualizing it."*

Cynthia pictured every single detail in her mind, even down to what clothes she had on. She visualized herself wearing a lime-green blouse when she won. And guess what?! She was wearing that exact blouse. *"That part kept surprising me,"* she says, laughing. *"I thought I'd lose weight by then and wouldn't still have that top."*

"When I found out, I sat in silence for a minute because it confirmed how powerful our minds can be," she says with a grin. *"Then I started screaming and crying!"* When asked what Cynthia would do if she lost the money, she said, *"I would simply visualize it again and make it happen."*

There are several interviews with Cynthia, most of which you can see on You Tube. This powerful lady is truly an inspiration.

One condition for successful visualization is persistence. I cannot stress how important this is. If you visualize for 5 minutes a day, twice a week, do you think you'll see results? Probably not. The Cynthia Stafford's and Arnold Schwarzenegger's in this world made visualization part of their daily life. Their mindset didn't waiver. You need to visualize your goal at least once a day, every single day.

Another important point to mention is never worry about the *How*. How will I get the money? How will it come to me? How will I win the competition? Do not, under any circumstances, worry about the *How*. This is the job of the Universe. If you visualize your goal for 5 minutes and then spend the next 5 minutes wondering about how it will manifest itself into your life, then you are indirectly telling the Universe that you don't believe. Believe it is yours, believe you have it. Visualize and let go, trust in the Universe, it will never let you down.

How long does it take to visualize what I want?

This is probably the most common question on everyone's lips. Unfortunately I can't give you a specific time scale. The length of time it takes to manifest your goals depends on what the goal is, what your beliefs are about obtaining that goal, and how dedicated you are to the visualization process. I always recommend you start small. Try and visualize an extra $100 in your account this month, visualize meeting an old friend you haven't seen in a while, or visualize getting a free meal. When you start to see results, your confidence will grow and you can start manifesting bigger goals. If you feel that you can start off and manifest $112 million like Cynthia Stafford, then go for it! It can be done.

Believe + Visualize = Dreams Come True!

A Visualization Exercise:

Firstly, write down your goal. In this visualization, we are going to visualize an extra $100 in our bank accounts.

I like to write my visualizations in my LOA journal.

Write out:

I am so happy and grateful now that I have received an extra $100 in my bank account.

If you feel more comfortable writing out something else, please do so. Always remember, however, **it has already happened**. Don't write:

I am so happy and grateful now that $100 is manifesting its way into my life.

If something *is manifesting* then it will always be *manifesting* and will never have *manifested*.

Step One

Once you have your goal written down, get yourself into a comfortable position and relax. If you find that putting on a relaxing song makes you feel more peaceful, then do that. Make sure you are not disturbed; switch your phone off or put it on silent.

Step Two

Take several deep breaths. Inhale through your nose and exhale through your mouth. When taking deep breaths, always breathe from the pit of your stomach, fill your lungs with air and then release. I always take 20 deep breaths and while exhaling I say to myself "I am relaxed" over and over again.

Step Three

Start visualizing a $100 dollar bill. Hold it in your hand, feel the crisp paper, put the figure $100 on a cinema screen, make it huge. Imagine what you would do with the money, how would you spend it? Feel how happy and secure you are, knowing that you have that extra money. Be thankful to the Universe for giving you this gift of an extra $100. See your bank statement with an extra $100 in the balance. See $100 bills everywhere. Smile. Feel good. Smell the money. Believe it is yours.

Repeat Step Three for 5 minutes. To end the visualization, thank the Universe. Thank you, thank you, thank you!

Slowly open your eyes and let go. Repeat at least once a day, every single day until the magic happens!

Exercise 8

Declutter Your Mind

Before you start this exercise, I want you to take out a piece of paper and pen, and answer the following questions honestly:

When was the last time you decluttered your kitchen cupboards?

Do you regularly wear all the clothes in your wardrobe?

Can you find the hammer in your garage?

Did you take the 1 week old empty Starbucks cup out of the car?

Are you in a rut, are you bored with certain aspects of your life?

Answers will vary but I hope you can see where I am going with this. Your world and everything in it is a reflection of you. Your home is no exception.

You wake up in your home, you live in your home, you sleep in your home. It is very much a huge part of your life. The thing you need to ask yourself is, does it reflect your mind?

When you start your LOA journey you need to start with a clean slate. That is why I recommend decluttering your home. Your home needs to support and nurture your mind. It needs to inspire you, and make you want to experience new things.

My Mum always used to say "A decluttered room is a decluttered mind." As a teenager it used to drive me insane but, of course, she was right! Start clearing out the old and make way for the new! You will be inspired, you will find new interests, new hobbies, you will find a new passion for life, and you will indirectly allow the Universe to deliver new things to you, because you have the room.

I urge you to include this exercise in your journey. Start small, don't overwhelm yourself by doing up the whole house in a week. Decluttering years of junk will not take a week! Make it one of your 5 a day goals - Exercise 17. Each week, pick a certain area of your house, for example, on Saturday morning you are going to dedicate 2 hours to cleaning out your wardrobe.

The golden rule I follow is; if you haven't worn it or used it in 6 months to a year, then it goes. Pack up several bags and give them to your local charity shop, this in itself will make you feel fantastic because you are giving back and helping others.

The most amazing thing about this exercise is 3 fold:

1. You can include it in your 5 a day goals and scratch it off the list when completed, making you feel like you have achieved what you set out to.

2. You are decluttering your home and mind.

3. You are giving to charity.

Achieve + Declutter + Give Back = feeling good.

Exercise 9

Check Out My Big Check

I've yet to meet a person who does not like to receive checks, especially when they are unexpected!

LOA abundance checks are a great way of raising your vibration so you can align yourself with a check you wish to receive. Using blank cheque templates you can write out exactly what specific amount you would like to receive. Basically you are placing an order with the Universe, "I would like a check for $1,000,000.00 please."

If you Google "blank cheque templates" under images, you will see a variety of cheques you can use. Copy the cheque image and paste it into paint.

1. Make the check payable to you.

2. Fill in the date you would like to receive the check. Make it believable, it has to feel right. If you write out a check for $10 million and date it in a fortnight's time, do you truly believe this can happen? If so, then go for it. If you feel like you need a little longer to manifest a large amount like that then date it for 6 months or 3 years later, whatever rests comfortably with you.

3. Write out the amount you would like in the box on the right and write out the amount in words on the left hand side underneath your name.

4. The *For* section can either be left blank or filled in. I leave mine blank because I am leaving it up to the Universe to decide how it will come to me. If you wrote a book and would like a publishing deal then write in...*For a Publishing Contract.*

5. Some people like to sign it *The Universe* or *Almighty God* or *The Law of Attraction.* I actually like to use a made up name because it seems more real to me.

6. I would recommend you surround yourself with the check. Print off a few copies (in color). Attach one to your vision board, tape one to the side of the bedside locker, place one under your pillow, place one in your wallet, and save the image as your screensaver.

7. Meditate on the check before you sleep or first thing when you wake up. And then let it go.

8. You can add power to this exercise by writing out lists of items you will buy with the money, what charities you will help, and how you will help out your family and friends.

There is a great clip on You Tube showing Jim Carrey

explain to Oprah how he manifested $10,000,000 by using this technique. It is very inspiring.

Here is an example of a check that I have used in the past:

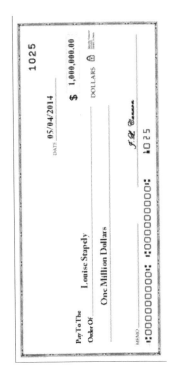

Exercise 10

Thank You Crystal

I'm sure the concept of carrying around a gratitude rock has been around for many years, but The Secret movie catapulted its popularity around the world.

Gratitude rocks come in many forms. You can purchase them online (there are some nice ones that have the word Gratitude written on the rock), you can use a small, smooth rock you found on the ground, you could use a sea shell picked up by your son or daughter, or you could use a crystal. Whatever touches your heart more.

Carry the rock with you throughout your day, put it in your purse, jacket pocket or trouser pocket. Each time you touch it, which could be a dozen times a day, give thanks for something that happened to you on that day.

Some examples:

I am grateful for getting into work on time.
I am grateful the traffic was good this morning.
I am grateful for getting that new deal.
I am grateful the weather is so lovely today.

I am grateful for feeling healthy and strong.
I am grateful for a lovely night's sleep last night.
I am grateful my family are healthy and happy.
I am grateful to have 2 hands so I can touch my
gratitude rock.

Being reminded of how grateful you are throughout
your day will bring more wonderful experiences into
your life that will make you feel even more thankful and
grateful. It is law.

Exercise 11

No News is Good News

The concept of the LOA is very simple; **what we focus on or give our attention to, we attract into our lives**. It is essential, therefore, that we make an effort to surround ourselves with positive people, positive situations, and positive stories.

Unfortunately today's media inundates us with their headlines every hour of every day from over a dozen channels, most of those headlines being sensationally negative.

This can be a very difficult exercise for some but if you are serious about practicing the LOA, eliminate news and newspapers for 30 days. Obviously if you are a business person you will want to keep informed of current market situations, but stay clear of the front page headlines about murder and mayhem. Being 100% honest with you, if I lived on my own, I would never watch the news. I haven't bought a newspaper in years and I have no desire to.

About 3 weeks ago, I watched the news with my boyfriend. The first 2 headlining stories were absolutely horrific and really upset me. I came away from that 30 minutes feeling completely depressed and very angry at how some people can treat others. I told my boyfriend that I was never going to watch the news again, he told me I was being ridiculous. I asked him how those 30 minutes had benefited me. He told me I was now informed about what was going on in the world. I then asked him, now that I had been informed, how has that information benefited me? He couldn't answer. The simple fact was it hadn't benefited me, not one bit. It affected me in a negative manner and that is not beneficial for anyone.

I completely understand if you are emotionally attached to a story or if it personally affects you, then you will want to watch it. I am not saying avoid all news now and forever, just don't watch it all the time. My Mum used to watch the 1pm, 6pm, and 9pm news. All the same headlines, all the same negativity 3 times over!

Try it for a month and see how you go. No news is good news!

Exercise 12

I Can Afford That

———— ❦ ————

This is another simple, yet effective exercise that can be practiced every day.

When we start off on our LOA journey, more often than not, we need to change our mindset. I cringe when I think of the amount of times I used to say "*I can't afford that*." No wonder I was broke all the time!

Even if you only have a dime in your purse, every single time you think of something you'd like, you see something advertised on TV, or you pass by something that you'd like to own, declare to yourself "*I can afford that*". It doesn't matter what it is; a car, a house, a pair of earrings, a pair of socks, you CAN afford it. Imagine yourself buying it, handing over cash for it, imagine that feeling of having it.

Change your internal affirmations from negative to positive. Eliminate the words *I can't afford it* from your vocabulary. Do this from now on, every day. You will be amazed at the results!

Exercise 13

Loose Lips Sink Ships

How many of you gossip about other people from time to time? My hand is up! Although I have become much more conscious of it since learning about the LOA.

When you talk about someone behind their back, you are judging that person, complaining about them or sometimes being bitchy towards them. Based on the LOA (which is working every second of every day), what do you think will be returned to you? Empathy? Kindness? Positive situations? I think not!

We've all done it, and I know it can brighten up a conversation and make it exciting, but the repercussions on a universal level are just not worth it.

When someone starts talking to you about another person, just pretend you have to go somewhere or make a call. You could ask that person not to speak to you about others or you could be more direct and tell that person that they shouldn't be gossiping about others. The more you do this and the more you avoid gossiping, the more it will become part of your past, you will no longer attract people who want to gossip.

Years ago, I worked in a life assurance company. About 2 years into it, a new girl started whom I became friendly with. She loved gossip and was very bitchy about her co-workers. Ashamedly, I joined in. Before I knew it, there were about 5 of us in this group, all with similar characteristics. This went on for about 2 years until I started learning about myself after coming across Louise Hay's book, *You Can Heal Your Life*. I was so disgusted at my actions. I realised I had attracted these people into my life and began the process of changing how I viewed myself and others.

The first thing I needed to do was step away from these people. I couldn't have them in my life. I began to distance myself. I stopped going on lunch with them, made excuses when there were nights out, and after a while the bitchiness turned on me! It hurt me because they totally turned their backs on me and were very mean. I can honestly say though that it was the best thing that ever happened to me and I'm so proud of myself for being strong enough to walk away. Because I did, I became friendly with another lovely girl who is my best friend to this day, she's a treasure and I love her dearly.

Don't gossip or bitch about others, feel and surround yourself with love, it will come back to you tenfold.

Exercise 14

Money Attracts Money

———————— ❦ ————————

This is a popular exercise among LOA'ers, and is used by thousands worldwide! I first discovered it when I read some books by Abraham-Hicks. I really liked the idea.

The main principle behind the LOA is you get what you think about most. If you think about not being able to afford things then that is what you will attract, not being able to afford things. One way to overcome this is to carry around a $20, $50, or $100 bill in your wallet, at all times. Try and have the highest denomination you can, this will make you feel more abundant.

You will not be physically spending the money, but mentally spending it one hundred times over. Every time you see something you'd like, think to yourself, *I can afford that, I have the money in my wallet.* And mentally buy it. The more you do this, the more your vibrations will resonate with wealth. Imagine how many times you could spend it! If I went shopping for the day and could spend $50 as many times as I'd like, I'd probably have to hire a trunk to carry everything home for me, how fun is that!

This exercise puts you in the state of feeling rich, and that is a state you want to keep. Once you feel rich and wealthy, the Universe will deliver more things to make you feel rich and wealthy.

Exercise 15

5 Goals a Day Keeps the Universe at Play

We've spoken about long term goal setting and how important it is if you want to be successful. Short term goal setting is no different. There is something so satisfying about achieving our goals. You feel like you have accomplished something significant, and it is that positive feeling that continues to raise your vibrations.

For this exercise you will need your daily journal. Every night, before you go to sleep, write out 5 goals that must be completed by the end of the next day. Because they are short term goals they must be achievable in one day. Here are some examples of goals I have listed:

- ❖ Clean out the spare room cupboard.
- ❖ Confirm my appointment at the doctors.
- ❖ Call Pam and ask her and Josh over for dinner next Saturday.
- ❖ Finish Chapter 3 in my exam question's book.
- ❖ Write out my Christmas cards.
- ❖ Buy stamps.
- ❖ Watch my mind movie twice.
- ❖ Call Mum & Dad to see how they are.
- ❖ Buy Megan's Birthday present.

Every night, before you get into bed, open up your journal and cross off every goal that you have completed.

Please try and complete all 5, I promise you, you will feel fantastic if you do. When you are finished, write out your next 5 goals for the following day. Continue this for 30 days, and once you build momentum, that satisfying feeling of achievement will make its way back to you in so many glorious ways.

Exercise 16

Affirmations

Affirmations are simple statements repeated to yourself silently or aloud, ones that can be either positive or negative. Every thought we think and word we say is creating our future, whether we know it or not. Negative affirmations create limitations in our life, positive affirmations create unlimited joyful experiences. Which would you choose?

Whatever you say by the conscious mind is accepted as true by the subconscious mind. So many of us affirm in a negative way on a daily basis.

I'm going to be late.
I am totally out of his league.
I'm not smart enough to learn that.
I'm sick and tired of him.

"I'm not, I'm not, I'm not. Every I'm not is a creation." - Fred Alan Wolfe.

How do we turn this around?

It starts with thinking differently, speaking differently, affirming differently. When we affirm positive words or

74

statements we make suggestions to our mind what we should be thinking. These positive suggestions attract more positive suggestions and so on, until the positive seed starts to take root.

Émile Coué, a French pharmacist and psychologist, believed in the power of positive affirmations, achieving phenomenal recovery rates in his clinics as a result. Dr. Coué taught each of his patients to say "Every day, in every way, I'm feeling better and better." He believed in the power of mindful autosuggestion.

The most beneficial time of the day to do affirmations is when you are between the state of wakefulness and sleep, during meditation, or when you are in a state of hypnosis. Affirmations can still be repeated when we are in a conscious state but please remember that the universe does not respond to words, it responds to vibration. You can repeat as many affirmations as you like, but if they are done in a routine manner with no emotion behind them, then in all likelihood you will not see the results you want.

Tips on doing affirmations:

1. You can do your affirmations in many ways. You can:

❖ Repeat them to yourself while feeling positive emotions.

❖ Repeat your affirmations on paper line after line while feeling positive emotions.

❖ Repeat your affirmations out loud while feeling positive emotions.

❖ Repeat your affirmations by typing out the same statement over and over while feeling positive emotions.

❖ Repeat your affirmations while meditating.

2. Ensure the affirmation is a short sentence, like a mantra. Make it simple and easy to remember and repeat. You will have much more success with:

I am financially abundant.

as opposed to

I am financially abundant and release any negative feelings I have about money. I allow money to come into my life. It is available to me in many ways. Money is easy to earn and I am constantly receiving easy money making ideas.

3. Always ensure that affirmations are in the present tense. Future tense statements such as *I will* make

money, will keep your desires exactly where you are stating...in the future.

4. Do not use the words *don't, not, no, never, can't, won't, couldn't, or shouldn't* in your affirmations.

Here are some of my favorite affirmations:

"Every day, in every way, my life is getting better and better."

"I love myself just the way I am."

"All is good in my world."

"I am surrounded by love and happiness."

"I am financially free."

"I am healthy, wealthy, strong, and happy."

Exercise 17

Story Telling

I absolutely love hearing about other people's LOA success. I honestly don't think there is better motivation than hearing how someone manifested their perfect partner or a million dollar check or better health. It is so lovely to hear.

More often than not, your LOA journey will take discipline, and lots of it! Sometimes, you will need to remind yourself of the wonderful possibilities that life holds. I do this by reading other people's success stories.

On The Secret Movie's website, there are literally thousands of success stories on a variety of topics including money, success, better health, physical appearance, marriage, love, friendship, exam success, and many more.

If you are having a demotivated day, spend 10 minutes reading some of these stories. They will instantly raise your vibration, and motivate you to get back on the LOA pathway. I recently read the story below and just had to share it with you. Talk about motivation!

"I had been introduced to The Secret years ago but never truly understood or appreciated it's true power until this past week.

About 3 weeks ago I started a new job. During training we watched the first 20 minutes of The Secret. I was motivated once again. I came home and told my girlfriend let's watch The Secret tonight. And so now, with open mind and heart, we watched the video and we were both moved to tears.

I immediately began putting The Secret into action.

Since Rhonda and I have been dating for 9 months we kept talking about going on a Windstar cruise, but it was all talk and the conversation was us usually talking about how we couldn't afford it.

After watching The Secret I went to my computer and we picked the exact trip we wanted to go on and printed the itinerary and placed it on the fridge. I also changed the background photo on my phone, iPad and computer to a picture of the ship. And we began to visualize ourselves not only on the trip, but on the deck relaxing.

This week, two amazing things have occurred.

First in regards of my new job, in which during training we watched The Secret and began this rekindled motivation. In the last 3 weeks I have the highest sales of the company and have been given a company car and

*credit card to pay for all gas and expenses along with a
bonus which will allow me to pay off my debt faster.*

*The second and even more incredible thing is that we
received a phone call from my parents with the following
statement. "Your father and I are going on a cruise to
celebrate our 50th anniversary and renew our vows and we
would like you and Rhonda to join us".*

*Oh, and by the way, this was the exact ship and cruise of
the itinerary that I had printed and placed on the fridge
and put photos on my computer, phone and iPad.*

Amazing things are, and will continue to happen.

*I am so grateful for the person that re introduced me to The
Secret and allowed me the chance to rediscover what was
already there, because my life has been changed forever and
there is no looking back.*

Thank you! Thank you! Thank you!"

Isn't that a great story?!

If you log onto www.thesecret.tv, there are tons more
stories like this one to inspire and motivate you.

Exercise 18

Change Your Day, Write Your Day

You will need your journal for this exercise. If you have a bad day, although I don't like to use the term 'bad day' so we'll change that.....if you have a day that could have gone better, take out your journal before bedtime and rewrite your day. It's as simple as that. Write down exactly how you would have liked your day to have gone.

So instead of:

Everything was going good this morning until I got stuck in traffic! I shouldn't have gone that route, what a stupid thing to do. Work was ok, I wish I had gotten one more case finished though, I'll be behind tomorrow now, oh well. Watched a good movie tonight, the kids went off to sleep ok. Mike drove me insane though, why does he have to have an opinion on every part of the movie, he really bugs me sometimes.

Write this:

I got to work on time this morning which was great, I always take the right route, the traffic was so light. Work was really productive, I managed to get an extra case done today so that means I can get off work early tomorrow! I had great fun with Mike and the kids tonight, we played monopoly and had such fun, I won of course!! Mike and I finished the night off with a lovely glass of wine and a great movie. I had a lovely day.

The idea behind this exercise is to try and keep your positive energy flowing, even if you've had a challenging day. Eventually you will find that the more you practice the LOA, the more infrequent those challenging days become.

Before you drift off to sleep visualize how your journal day went, and say:

Thank You!

Exercise 19

The Focus Wheel

This is a very effective Abraham Hick's process that will help you release any resistance you may have on a particular subject.

The process of the LOA involves deliberate creation, and in order to deliberately create something in your life, you need to focus on that something in a positive manner. I cannot tell you the amount of times I have started using the LOA in my life only to get distracted after 1 or 2 weeks and lose focus. And I know for a fact I'm not on my own. You need to focus on whatever it is you want to manifest in your life, every single day. The Focus Wheel is a fantastic tool for you to use to do just that.

The Focus Wheel causes you to change your vibrational point of attraction (how you feel) on any subject, whether it is a bad relationship or lack of money. For the purpose of this exercise I'm going to use a bad relationship with Mike as an example. If you love your significant other but are not getting along, it means your current vibration is one of low energy or negative energy, and as a result, you will attract more of the same. You need to focus on changing this vibration.

As hard as it may seem sometimes, it can be done.

The idea behind the Focus Wheel is to help you improve your feeling of clarity, and shift your focus away from not being happy to being happy. I have attached an image below that will give you an idea of how your Focus Wheel should look. If you Google "Focus Wheel Law of Attraction" under images, you will find more great examples.

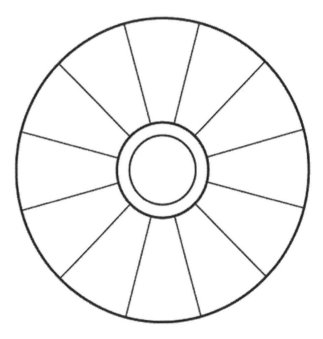

Firstly, identify what it is you DON'T want and write it outside the wheel.

In this case, *I am fed up fighting with Mike so much. I don't want to feel annoyed with him anymore.*

Now in the center of the wheel, make your statement of intent, for example, **"Harmonious relationship with Mike."**

In each of the segments surrounding the circle, make a positive statement, one that you already believe closely matches your desire, not one that offers up any resistance. For example, does Mike bring you flowers every Friday? If you answer no but you would like him to, then putting a statement such as "Mike brings me flowers every Friday" will offer up great resistance because it simply isn't true.

After you complete the Focus Wheel, your aim is to be left in a better feeling place by improving your point of attraction (in this case, harmonious relationship).

The closest statements I found which did not offer up any resistance were:

❖ I am happy in the knowledge that the harmonious relationship I desire is there for my discovery.

85

- ❖ I'm looking forward to making this change.

- ❖ I know there are other couples out there who have overcome their differences.

- ❖ I am filled with love when I think of the beautiful children we created together.

- ❖ I smile when I remember our relationship at the beginning.

- ❖ I love the feeling of being loved.

- ❖ It will be really fun to laugh with Mike again.

- ❖ I know that relationships offer up some challenges but those challenges make us stronger.

- ❖ I love it when myself and Mike hold hands.

- ❖ I know that, sometimes in relationships, stubbornness can overshadow love.

- ❖ I really enjoy it when myself and Mike are getting along harmoniously.

- ❖ I know there is still love in the relationship, I know we will be fine.

Here is my finished Focus Wheel which I completed in Microsoft Paint:

The feeling I felt when I wrote outside the wheel, compared to the feeling I felt after I finished the wheel, was significantly better and more positive. None of those statements above conflicted with how I felt, if they did, it would be a waste of time including them, as they would make me feel resistance.

By doing this exercise I have now shifted my vibration from one of negativity to one of positivity and hope.

Even if all you feel is hope, that is a great start.

Because of this change in my point of attraction, I will now start to attract more circumstances that match my new positive vibration.

Tips on The Focus Wheel

1. You can do a Focus Wheel on absolutely anything you want - money, relationships, friendship, a better job, a harmonious relationship with your boss, better health, physical appearance, and many more.

2. I recommend saving a blank focus wheel from Google (like I did in the example I showed you) and print out about 30 of them. Do one every day for 1 week. You can do 30 Focus Wheels on the same subject, or any subject that is bothering you on a particular day.

3. The most important point to remember is to always write out statements that do not create any feelings of resistance towards the subject.

4. There is an App called Focus Wheel that you can download for free. It is fun and really easy to use.

Exercise 20

Seeing Is Believing - Believing Is Seeing

Whatever material desire it is you choose, you must apply attention to it, you must act as if you already have it. One way to do this is to shop for it. Even if your current external circumstances state that you have no money, your internal circumstances state that you are very wealthy and can afford nice things.

Remember, your subconscious believes what you show it, it will attract according to your thoughts.

- ❖ If you desire a new car, go to a show room and test drive it. When driving the car, feel how excited you are, smell the leather seats, feel how it feels to have your hands wrapped around the steering wheel, listen to the engine. Test drive as many cars as you can, go to different show rooms.

- ❖ View million dollar houses in the area of your choice. Imagine how you would feel if you lived there, look at the beautiful furnishings, the lovely decor, and feel how rich it is.

- ❖ If you'd love to get engaged, try on engagement rings, get your ring finger measured, and take a photo of your hand with the ring on.

- ❖ Go to wedding fairs and exhibitions. Go to the hotel where you would like to get married and speak to the wedding planner, ask to be shown around.

- ❖ Try on expensive shoes, try on expensive clothing. Feel how soft the material is, smell the leather on the shoes, look at yourself in the mirror. Even takes photos of yourself in the dressing room.

- ❖ Go to the Marina and look at boats, go to boat shows, get free brochures online.

  If you inject yourself into a life of plenty then that is what you will attract. It is important however, not to experience feelings of want or envy when you are viewing the house or car of your dreams, this will only attract more circumstances that will result in you 'wanting' or 'envying'.

  Imagine yourself as a success and that is what you will attract.

Exercise 21

Spend, Spend, Spend

───────────── ⟡ ─────────────

This is a popular exercise introduced by Abraham Hicks called The Prosperity Game. The idea behind it is:

Every day for 1 month you will receive a check from the Universe that doubles its amount each day. If you start on a Monday, for example, you will receive a check for $1,000, on Tuesday you'll receive $2,000, Wednesday $4,000, Thursday $8,000, and so on. When I tried to calculate how much you would get on day 30, there wasn't enough room on my calculator for the zeros. I think it was $536,870,912,000, $536 billion?! Even if I physically had $536 billion, it would take some serious imagination to spend it and would probably take weeks!! For me, the exercise had now become a chore.

Starting on $100 brought me to just over $53 billion. Even that seemed like a chore.

"Playing a game that feels like work is no longer serving its purpose." - Abraham Hicks

For this reason, I started on $10 per day. It might seem like a small figure to start out on, but by day 30 I had $5,368,709,120, just a little over $5 billion! I had a huge portfolio of properties around the world, I had every toy you could image, I had a fabulous collection of super cars, and an enviable yacht at every port.

To take this exercise a step further, create a folder on your computer and call it "The Prosperity Game." Inside that folder, create a further 30 folders, and name them $10, $20, $40, and so on. Find images of what you would purchase each day, and save them in each corresponding folder. Now you can actually see what you have purchased.

Receiving the checks can be done in a few different ways:

❖ Print off 30 blank checks, fill them out and place the correct amount under your pillow each night. In the morning, open the check and write out everything you will buy that day.

❖ If you have any old check books lying around, write out a daily check for yourself, and place it under your pillow each night.

❖ Open up a new page in your journal every morning, and write the daily amount on the top of the page. Imagine holding a check for that amount. List everything you will purchase that day.

❖ If you prefer using the computer, build an online spreadsheet. Make a list of the amounts and put your purchases beside each amount.

❖ There is an online prosperity game that I have read about. I haven't used it so I can't give my opinion on it but it looks good, and is free to use once you register. It says that you can design blank checks, record your purchases, receive emails with increasing deposits for a year, and have access to a member's only group where you can share your experiences and successes. If you Google "Free Prosperity Game" you will find it in the first couple of results.

Tips on using The Prosperity Game:

❖ Don't just routinely make lists every morning. You need to imagine how you would FEEL when you are purchasing each item. Imagine handing over the money. Imagine handling or using the product.

❖ Don't give money away to friends, family, or charities as this is creating a feeling of lack for those concerned. Everyone has the ability to create whatever amount of money they choose. See your respective others as being abundant.

❖ Don't put any money in a savings account.
This creates a feeling of 'saving for a rainy day'
or 'saving for the future in case you need it.'
That is the wrong message to give the Universe.
You are now the deliberate creator of your life,
and as a result, you will always have more than
enough money for the future.

❖ Start off on whatever amount you feel
comfortable with. I chose $10 because it
resonated with me personally. Using $1,000
will give you over $530 billion on day 30, $100
will give you over $53 billion, $10 will give you
over $5 billion, and starting off on $1 will give
you $536,870,912!

❖ You don't have to do this game for 30 days, if
those amounts of money above are still too big
for you on day 30, then do the exercise for 15 or
20 days.

Exercise 22

Books & Movies

Initially when I started on my LOA journey, I sometimes needed little reminders to keep me focused and motivated. I found books and movies great ways to do this.

I always have an LOA book by my bed. Even though I have read most of the books out there, I still feel that you can learn something new. Before I do my LOA exercises at night, I open the book randomly at any page, and read for about 5 minutes. Sometimes in the morning, if I'm feeling a little deflated, I do the same.

I regard myself as a visual creature, I like to see images rather than imagine them. That is why I absolutely love watching LOA movies. I will try and watch 2 movies per week, one at the start of the week and the other towards the end. Again, they keep me focused and motivated, just like the LOA books.

My favorite movies are:

The Secret
You Can Heal Your Life by Louise Hay
Leap

The Opus
Introducing Abraham - The Secret Behind the Secret
What the Bleep Do We Know
The Compass
Beyond Belief

The ones I watch regularly are The Secret, You Can Heal Your Life, Introducing Abraham, and What the Bleep, all fantastic movies.

To get an idea of what these movies are like, there are clips of each one on You Tube, this will allow you to get a feel for what movie is right for you.

Various movies and books have touched me pretty deeply, and have helped with my own personal development throughout the years. They have allowed me to understand the intricacies of the LOA, and have kept my journey fun and exciting. I hope they will do the same for you.

Exercise 23

Monopolise Your Wealth

I once read about a lady who used Monopoly money to change her feelings towards money, and therefore attract more abundance into her life. I was intrigued by the idea so decided to give it a go, and boy was I surprised with the results. At the beginning of my LOA journey (when I didn't have spare cash), I carried large denomination monopoly notes in my wallet. My wallet was literally bulging with them. Every day, at least once per day, I would take the money out and count it, at all times feeling like it was real actual money. I did this for about 3 months.

I no longer use this method now as I have enough real money to carry around in my wallet. It was one of several exercises I did at the beginning, to focus my point of attraction on bringing more money into my life. Although a very simple exercise, I truly believe it helped me attract more abundance into my life.

Start doing this today. Each time you count your money, affirm to yourself:

I have plenty of money, my wallet is always full, and I have enough money to buy whatever I choose.

Exercise 24

I Can't, I Won't, I Don't, I'm Not

⸺⸺⸺⸺⸺ ⚭✕⚭ ⸺⸺⸺⸺⸺

The very first self-help book I read was called, *You Can Heal Your Life* by Louise Hay. It completely opened my eyes on how I was speaking *to* myself *about* myself. Before I read the book I constantly criticized myself and my actions, I had very little self worth, and loving myself was the furthest thing from my mind. It has been an uphill battle with my internal demons but I've managed to eliminate 90% of the negative self talk. If I'm having a bad day, a little negativity creeps in from time to time but I've learned to accept that for what it is, acknowledge it, and move on to a more positive thought (this is where Exercise 23 - The Focus Wheel can change your point of attraction).

Negative self-talk can have such a detrimental effect on our self-esteem and confidence, it is imperative that we stop. Various books I have read on the topic of self-talk, claim that we think anywhere between 50,000 and 70,000 thoughts per day. Let's say you have 60,000 every day, how many of those thoughts do you think are positive and how many are negative? One way to answer that question is to take a look around you, look at your life, your bank balance, your partner, and your health. Are things going well in these areas of your life?

Your external circumstances reflect your internal thoughts. I can safely say that probably about 80% of my daily thoughts were negative, and that really frightened me in the beginning. I had to change. The following statements are examples of some of the opinions I used to have about myself:

- ❖ I can't afford that.
- ❖ I won't be able to do it.
- ❖ My memory isn't good.
- ❖ I'm not brainy enough.
- ❖ I definitely couldn't do that.
- ❖ I can't do it.

I shudder when I think back to the number of times those statements went through my head. As I said before, it was an uphill battle at the beginning, but I eventually eliminated them.

Other statements that need to be forgotten are:

- ❖ I'm so stupid.
- ❖ How are you? I'm not bad.
- ❖ The weather isn't bad today.
- ❖ I'm so angry.
- ❖ He makes me so mad.
- ❖ That's not fair.
- ❖ Why aren't there any normal men/women out there?
- ❖ Men are bastards.

- ❖ Women are a pain in the ass.
- ❖ I can't lose weight.
- ❖ Diets don't work.
- ❖ I'm not good enough.
- ❖ I'm going to be late.
- ❖ This is horrible.
- ❖ Oh my God, that's terrible.
- ❖ Life's a bitch.
- ❖ Typical.
- ❖ If it can go wrong, it will go wrong.

I could fill this book with the negative self-talk that we inflict on ourselves on a daily basis, but I won't, you get the idea. Thinking negatively about ourselves is a habit, and any habit, with time and practice, can be changed. When you catch yourself saying something you shouldn't, stop, breathe and say the exact opposite.

New Positive Statments:

- ❖ I can afford it.
- ❖ I can do whatever I set my mind to.
- ❖ Everything happens for a reason.
- ❖ I can do it.
- ❖ I remember things easily.
- ❖ I have the ability to learn.
- ❖ How are you? I'm good thanks, or I'm great thanks.
- ❖ I'm going to make it on time.

❖ I can lose weight.

Tips on eliminating negative self-talk:

1. Don't beat yourself up each time you catch yourself saying something negative. Just acknowledge it and let it go. You need to realise that habits take time to change.

2. Eliminate the following: *I can't, I'm not, not bad, not good.*

3. Each time you think a negative thought, take a deep breath, release the thought from your mind, and replace it with the complete opposite. So for example:

"I'll never be able to learn this."

Becomes;

"I am able and willing to learn this, I allow myself to learn this."

Exercise 25

Scrap That Idea

⎯⎯⎯⎯⎯⎯⎯⎯⎯ ⟡ ⎯⎯⎯⎯⎯⎯⎯⎯⎯

This is one of my favourite exercises that I do from time to time, especially when I want to attract something specific into my life. It is so effective and so much fun, I urge you to include it as part of your LOA journey.

When you have a desire, create a scrapbook on the subject. While scrapbooking is similar to vision boards, the one significant difference is the focus of intent. Vision boards contain many different images of various things you would like to attract into your life. A scrapbook on the other hand, contains many images of one particular subject, for example, a house or car. When you focus all of your creative energies on one thing at a time, it supercharges the manifestation process at an accelerated speed.

When you create a scrapbook you are working with beautiful color and imagery that invoke powerful emotions of love and appreciation, and it is these emotions that will ultimately result in successful manifestation.

The great thing about scrapbooking is there are no rules. You can choose whatever images you like. Go to craft shops and buy stickers or glitter or fancy paper, whatever you choose. You get back what you put in!

Tips on how to create your scrapbook:

❖ The most important aspect to creating a scrapbook is to have a clear, specific idea of what it is you want to attract. "I want a new home" is too general, be more specific like, "I want to create a new home by the sea. It has 4 double bedrooms with great sea views. There is a small wooden stairway down to the beautiful white sand."

❖ Find images you would like to include in your scrapbook. What color do you want your house to be? What layout? How many bedrooms? What color would you like the walls to be? What color kitchen? What size bed do you want for the master bedroom? What color and design is your bathroom suite? Do you have a walk in wardrobe?

❖ There are so many decor and homeware websites out there that offer free brochures and magazines, use these to find the images you wish to include in your scrapbook.

❖ Dedicate one or more pages per room and underneath your images write out exactly how you want that room to look.

❖ Draw out your own floor plan on an A4 blank sheet of paper. Put the rooms, windows, and doors exactly where you want them to be.

❖ If there is a specific house or specific area in which you want to live, write out the address on every page.

This can become a lovely meditative experience, and as you know, once the mind is in a quiet space it is more open to receiving.

Exercise 26

Letter Of Love

As we discussed in Exercise 2 - Attitude of Gratitude, applying the principle of gratitude to our daily lives, brings about magical experiences.

At the end of every week, take out some writing paper, and write a thank you letter to the Universe. When you finish, place it in an envelope, address it to The Universe, and place it in your nearest post box. You don't need to put any stamp on it, trust that the Universe will receive it. Here is an example of a letter I once wrote:

Dear Universe

I have had the most wonderful week and would like to thank you in every way for making it happen.

Thank you for a productive week on my book. I loved every minute of it, particularly the progress I made.

Thank you for making Murphy's appointment at the vet a success.

Thank you for allowing me to experience the magic of a

Christmas tree, I love when I see the lights come on.

Thank you for the food you provided me with this week, I had lovely meals and am very blessed to be able to eat when I please.

Thank you for providing me with plenty of money to buy Mum's Birthday present, she absolutely loved it.

Thank you for providing me with a quiet space so I can learn and grow in my Law of Attraction journey.

Thank you for creating a harmonious home with Mike. We laughed together a lot this week.

Thank you for a wonderful week.

I love and cherish you, now and forever.

Louise.xxx

Because there is a chance your letter might be opened by a curious mail man, don't put any names on it, simply substitute the name for "my dog" or "my husband" or "my partner."

Place yourself in an attitude of gratitude as much as you possibly can. You will reap the most amazing rewards.

Exercise 27

Friends Like These

Being surrounded by like-minded people who share similar interests in the LOA can be very beneficial to your journey. Have you ever been to a LOA seminar and felt the energy in the room? It is exhilarating. Now imagine having that on a regular basis!

Shortly after the release of The Secret, my friends and I started our Secret Group. We met up every Tuesday evening, and discussed what we had achieved that week and what our goals were going to be for the next week. We shared stories, shared our successes, and asked for advice on certain areas if we needed it. I created my first vision board at our meetings, it was such a lovely experience.

Join a LOA group or start one yourself. Attending regular meetings is a great way to keep you focused and an even better way to meet people. Like-minded people will inspire you, empower you, encourage you to be everything you can be, they will show you ways to make your dreams come true, appreciate your journey, and motivate you to find true happiness.

Here is a link to a great website that has details of LOA

Meet Ups around the world, hopefully you can find one near you.

www.lawofattraction.meetup.com

Exercise 28

Tap to Success

EFT or Emotional Freedom Technique has become a hugely popular therapy over the last few years, and is now widely regarded as an essential LOA tool.

Designed by Gary Craig, EFT is a gentle form of psychological acupressure that helps to return the body and mind to a natural state of balance and harmony by gently tapping on certain acupuncture points on the body, whilst repeating certain relevant phrases at the same time.

EFT, also called tapping, helps people to address certain emotional problems or physical discomforts such as:

Insomnia
Fear of water
Fear of flying
Fear of public speaking
Grief
Weight loss
Anxiety Attacks
Physical Pain
Limiting Beliefs

Besides lack of focus and persistence, what do you think is the second most popular reason for failure at attracting the life of your dreams using the LOA? Limiting beliefs. You will never attract money into your life if, deep down, you believe you don't deserve it.

Why do we have limiting beliefs?
As difficult as this can be for some people to hear, most of our beliefs have come from our parents, guardians, and teachers. Our fundamental beliefs are recorded in our subconscious before we are 7 years old and shape our habits of perception and behaviour throughout our lives. The following are some examples of messages that we hear during childhood:

- ❖ Money is hard to come by.
- ❖ You have to work hard to get money.
- ❖ Rich people walk all over you.
- ❖ You are your own worst enemy.
- ❖ You are not smart enough.
- ❖ Life can be tough sometimes.
- ❖ That's life.
- ❖ You'll never amount to anything.
- ❖ You're worthless.
- ❖ Only smart people can be successful.

Growing up believing even one of these limiting beliefs will have a detrimental effect on particular areas of your life. In order to determine what beliefs you have, ask yourself the following questions:

- ❖ Do you believe earning money is hard work?
- ❖ Do you believe you deserve to have money?
- ❖ Do you believe there is enough money for everyone?
- ❖ Do you believe you are worth loving?
- ❖ Do you believe you deserve to have a happy relationship?
- ❖ Do you believe you deserve to be happy?
- ❖ Do you believe you are smart enough to be successful?

If you have answered *No* to any of these questions, then whatever negative belief you have needs to be changed. Trying to attract a loving, harmonious marriage into your life is impossible when, deep down you don't believe you are good enough.

The above limiting beliefs need to be changed to:

- ❖ I believe that earning money is easy.
- ❖ I deserve to have money, I deserve to be rich.
- ❖ I believe there is enough money in the world for everyone.
- ❖ I deserve to be in a happy relationship.
- ❖ I deserve to be loved.
- ❖ I am worthy.
- ❖ I deserve the best in life.
- ❖ I deserve to be loved.

- ❖ I am smart.
- ❖ I am capable.
- ❖ I can do it.
- ❖ I am good enough.

EFT is an extremely effective way to change limiting beliefs. As I mentioned above, there are certain acupressure points used in this therapy. If you see the image on the next page, you will see the 9 points used in EFT:

Tapping Points

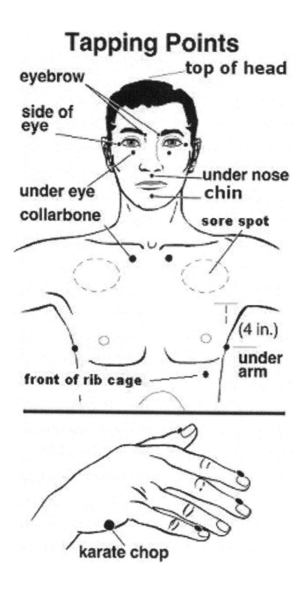

How to perform an EFT treatment:

1. Determine what negative emotion is holding you back, and then identify the intensity of that emotion on a scale between 0 and 10 (10 being intense). For example, *I find it hard to earn money*. On a scale of 0 to 10, how strongly do you feel the emotion of finding it hard to earn money?

2. Start off by acknowledging how you feel by saying: "Even though I find it hard to earn money, I totally and completely love and accept myself anyway." This is often called a Setup Phrase. Say this 3 times while gently tapping the karate chop point.

3. Next identify several reminder phrases regarding the emotion, some examples include:

- ❖ I am frustrated that I am not earning enough money.
- ❖ I don't know why I can't figure it out.
- ❖ I worry about not having enough money.
- ❖ I envy those who have enough money.

This step will be very personal to you. You don't necessarily have to have a script before you start, you can just tap on whatever emotion arises as you continue the exercise.

4. Tap through all the points in the image above while

repeating your reminder statements. Tap in the following order:

- ❖ Inner eyebrow.
- ❖ Outer eye, temple area.
- ❖ Under the eye, below the center of the eye.
- ❖ Under the nose, between the lip and nose.
- ❖ On the chin, in the center where the crease is.
- ❖ On your collarbone (either side is fine).
- ❖ Under your arm, about 2 - 3 inches below the crease of your armpit.
- ❖ Top of the head, right at the center of the crown.

5. Repeat this round of tapping again (leaving out the karate chop).

6. When you have finished, rate your intensity of feeling on a scale of 0 to 10. Has it changed?

7. The problem will have either disappeared completely, reduced in intensity, remained the same, or increased in intensity.

8. If it has remained the same or increased in intensity, repeat another round of tapping and see what other emotions come up. Often we remember instances in our childhood where we were given certain messages, for example, did your Mum or Dad ever say that you have to work really hard to earn money?

My friend introduced me to tapping about 3 years ago and since then, I have found it an incredible tool to overcome certain emotions and beliefs. I have tapped on several emotions regarding my body, relationships, money, and health. I even tapped before an exam once as I was so so nervous. It really worked too! I felt so calm and collected during the exam, and passed with flying colors.

When you are tapping don't be surprised if an emotion comes up that you had no idea was the cause of your resistance. My friend actually tapped regarding her breast size because her small breasts had always made her life a misery. While tapping, she remembered as a child her Mum saying to her that large breasts were only for large ladies. She realised that she had carried that belief with her throughout puberty, and because she wasn't overweight, her breasts didn't grow. Before she started EFT she was a 32AA, after 6 weeks, she grew 2 inches. This wasn't something that happened over night, she tapped on several hidden layers until she unravelled the true belief she held about her breasts.

There are several videos on You Tube showing the power of EFT, and how it can seriously make a difference on your journey.

Exercise 29

Sing to the Beat

Music is one of the best ways to instantly change your vibration as it has a powerful influence on your heartbeat, breathing, emotions, and feelings. Listening to music while you are visualizing can greatly increase the rate at which you manifest your desire.

I have created several playlists (with 8 songs each) for my MP3 player, incorporating songs that make me feel good and raise my vibration. They include:

1. A positive playlist with my favorite uplifting songs - I listen to this when I'm feeling down.

2. A love song playlist - I listen to this when I am visualizing my wedding and my relationship.

3. A meditative playlist - I listen to this when I have trouble meditating or when I want to quieten my mind.

4. A fast song playlist with my favorite upbeat songs - I listen to this when I am visualizing most parts of my life (money, house, car, friendships).

Always choose the right songs for you, making sure they

motivate and inspire the achievement of your desires.

Recommendation: If you are going to create a playlist for meeting the man/woman of your dreams, do not include songs that remind you of past relationships or breakups.

Exercise 30

Vision Boards

Vision boards shot to popularity after The Secret Movie, particularly after John Assaraf's story of manifesting his Dream Home in California, the exact home he cut out of a magazine and placed on his vision board.

"Knowing the law of attraction, I wanted to really put it to use and see what would happen so in 2005, I created a vision board. I put pictures of things I wanted to achieve and attract - like a car or a watch - up on this board. Every day I would sit in my office and I would look up at the board and I would start to visualize. I would really get into the state of already acquiring it.

After moving three times and ending up in California, I opened a box that included my vision boards. I cut open the box that had been packed away for five years, and on one vision board was a picture of a home I clipped from an old copy of Dream Homes Magazine. When I cut it out of the magazine, I hadn't known where it was located or how much it cost. But there was no mistaking it. It was a picture of the house I was sitting in at that very moment. Not a house like it. It was a unique house on 6 acres, with 188 windows, 320 orange trees, 2 lemon trees, and a slew

*of other special features. I actually bought my dream
home, renovated it and didn't even know it. I was blown
away. I finally understood the power of visualization."*

What is a vision board?

A vision board is a poster board on which you place
various images of items you would like to manifest into
your life. Popular images include;

- ❖ A car
- ❖ Your dream house
- ❖ A picture of a country you would like to visit
- ❖ A Rolex watch
- ❖ An engagement ring
- ❖ Meeting a person of influence

The idea behind it is to surround yourself with images
of what possessions you want to have, where you would
like to visit, who you would like to meet, and how
happy you would like to be. Each time you look at the
images, close your eyes and visualize already having
them in your life, feeling positive emotions of joy and
happiness.

How do I make a vision board?

1. The most important first step in making a vision
board is to have clear, concise goals written down in
your journal. I always write my vision board goals in
the present tense with specific details so I can visualize

them more clearly, for example:

I have a Lady Oyster Perpetual Rolex watch. It is 26mm, steel, silver in color, and has flat three-piece links. It fits me perfectly and looks lovely on my left wrist.

2. You can purchase a plain white poster board online from Ebay.com, Staples.com, or Amazon.com, or from any craft shop in your area. I use size A1 but you can use smaller if you wish (not too small though, you want your images to stand out). You can also use a cork board but I prefer poster boards as they are sturdier and come in the size I want.

3. Get your images from old/new magazines, websites, photos etc. Your brain thrives on images so make them as colorful and varied as you can. Also use images of words on how you want to feel, for example, cut out the words - Love, Success, Happiness, Joy, Excitement. You can also type out affirmations and print these off, for example, *I am making my dreams come true*, or I *am content and happy.* In the center of my vision board I have the words, *My Life*, in large bold print. These words clarify to me that the surrounding images are actually part of my life.

3. Once you have decided on your goals, written them down, and collated all images that correspond with these goals, glue them onto the poster board.

4. Place your vision board somewhere you will see it at least once per day. Mine is in my office at home and faces me while I work.

5. Each time you view your board, focus on the images and words, and visualize having them in your life.

Tips on making your vision board:

1. There are 2 types of vision boards you can create - 1. a collage of many images on several goals you have or, 2. a vision board on one specific theme. Focusing on one specific goal at a time can sometimes supercharge the manifestation process.

2. Before you create your vision board, make sure you have about 1 - 2 hours of uninterrupted time.

3. While practicing this exercise, put on some inspiring, uplifting music in the background. Don't forget the ability of music to evoke certain emotions in our bodies.

Vision boards are a fantastic way to focus attention on our desires, and add clarity to what we want to attract into our lives.

That's It!

You've come to the end of the exercises. I hope you have found some that will motivate and inspire you to create the life of your dreams.

I wish you all the very best of luck with your journey. Keep going and don't give up. Your dream life is waiting for you. Go get it!

Louise.xxx

68750118R00070

Made in the USA
Lexington, KY
19 October 2017